In Cannon Cave

In Cannon Cave

Carole Glasser Langille

Brick Books

CANADIAN CATALOGUING IN PUBLICATION DATA

Langille, Carole Glasser
In cannon cave

Poems.
ISBN 0-919626-91-2

I. Title.

PS8573.A55715 1997 C811'.54 C97-930513-6
PR9199.3.L315 1997

We acknowledge the support of the Canada Council for the Arts
for our publishing programme. The support of the Ontario Arts
Council is also gratefully acknowledged.

The cover photo of Riverport, Nova Scotia is by Terry James.
The author photo is courtesy of Sue Bookchin.

Typeset in Ehrhardt.
The stock is acid-free Zephyr Antique laid.
Printed and bound by The Porcupine's Quill Inc.

Brick Books
431 Boler Road, Box 20081
London, Ontario, N6K 4G6

In Memory of

Dr Charles William Avery
December 11, 1928 - December 12, 1974
with much gratitude

Contents

I

    You know the secret passageways
of the soul, the roads that dreams take,
and the calm evening
where they go to die ... There the good and silent spirits

    of life are waiting for you,
and one day will carry you
to a garden of eternal spring.

              Antonio Machado

Prayer

Every hour I am disappearing
where sun collides with icy leaves
and hovers in the brilliant air.
Trees light with a backdrop of winter.
Yellow grass smoulders under leaves.
I am being translated, painstakingly,
atom by atom, into everything that breathes.
Each winter I'm present –
the earth in vestments, a white sleeve
covering its bones. Do not disturb me.
I am walking deeper into the day
where sun slips between houses.
Wind leans into me as I lean against houses.
Soon night will cast off its thin clothes
and nestle down on earth as if earth
were a blanket, the evening deep in vespers,
the smell of moss, its green incantation.
Each hour relinquishes more light.
Soon the moon will rise and make its way forward
in this dark water, this intimacy
of quiet. It's as if the door were open and I,
resonant and indecipherable as evening,
were passing through.

3 a.m.

Something sparked the cinder of night
and lit it: cats fighting, a crow, the smell

of lemon geraniums flooding the evening.
Like a swimmer treading water, my body

floated on the surface of sleep
and would not sink. Here,

noises hidden from the sleeper.
Like an animal let loose in the wild,

a deeper part of me learns to do things for itself,
slowly. It knows the taste of cold water.

Here, sand warm where the sun shone all day,
silence like sweet berries

found in the forest.
Like birds that don't move forward

but circle round and back
there are moments that never leave, places

that send their messages through the cawing of birds.
Places that hint of clear lakes

where you can look deeply into water.
On a tightrope miles above everything I hoped for,

this is how I left one place
and entered another.

I learned to balance
by not touching the edges of my life.

What leaves even as it lingers?
What claims privacy for its own?

My task is to separate fear from the dream.
See the air I hold in my hands.

Looking At Houses

The dead look across the invisible world
and see how bright our world is

and bare. They see us best
by light streaming around us

until it thins and disappears.
Light that burns in dreams. Recently,

a dream I had: a house for sale. Sisters asking
two thousand dollars. Everything twinned.

One flight down
a picture window doubled.

Beyond, a frozen lake, ice reflecting sun.
The room aches with brightness.

But the curtain is drawn.
Always something held back. How will I pay?

When I woke, what remained – light.
And something else. 'Trust everything'

the dead warn us. 'The body
has good will.' Bright the voices.

Deep the tremors. Deep the bass of joy.
I remember turning down a shining road

the night the dead showed me houses.
Inside me, a room well lit. Land. Vastness.

Travel

Some nights a woman doesn't sleep.
She lies in bed while part of her
wanders streets in another city. She is trying
to tidy something up. In the morning
she's tired. That's when a woman is most susceptible
to voices. 'Close your eyes,' something tells her
and she does. When she opens them
half her life is gone.

When she visits
broken parts of herself, there is no direction. The ocean
can crash against a dream
and startle her. It's hard to find the way to dry land
in the dark. But after a while,
you learn the language of praise
in the dark. (Many things come
of their own accord if they're invited ... a violin concerto
drifting from the neighbour's house, waves pounding
on the beach at night.)
What is prayer, anyway?

Scanning an Afternoon in Winter

Earth is a cipher. I read
the ocean: light, dark. Dark
that feeds light running down
the wave's smooth mouth. Trough filled
with a slough of brown. Underbelly
rising. Then, rough as bark,
a spill of foam on shore. What?
Green weeds on sand in winter? This language
dragged up from the ocean floor. Waves swell
then collapse, their lapping sound repeating,
sibilant: whish, an*guish* ...
Sun retreats behind a thick lens then makes its way
down, the earth's belly hard.
If there's something I need to know –
earth, foam, water – *let* me know.
This inviolability floats
like ice on water in snow.

Winter

Apples frozen on trees –
little orange Chinese lanterns –
decorations for the party
of snow and quiet.

And in that quiet –
wildness. Can you hear the invitations?
The world kissing you,
brushing against you.

Hansel and Gretel

They broke night's back walking, vertebrae
hacked open to let day seep through.
Who hasn't been abandoned?

'My love' they imagined
in a voice whispered to a young child. What they heard,
what they felt, was absence: a cry in the mouth of the forest.

Even when they saw the house, they must have known
they couldn't rest. Known, hungry as they were,
that sweetness that camouflages other tastes.

What they learned, finally, is what everyone learns,
(as branches turned
to iron crutches): In time pain changes. But time –

what it takes it removes incompletely
the way a moonless night devours trees,
the way dark extinguishes a forest.

The wind gripped them. And they could hear it
as if it were speaking: *let go
of what you can; time doesn't want to be touched.*

The Little Things

Eventually everything leaves its name behind,
on the roads, in the towns, in the fallen leaves. Eventually,
we admit our failures, if only
because we want to see ourselves clearly as we are.

A splash of sun rolls up the hill
followed by a splash of shade
then sun again,
the very earth moved by its shadows. And we find
what reaches out to us
waits for us: the caress of a voice,
water quivering under a mooring. Everything
happening so quickly
and taking so long. And that's our luck – beauty a wave
about to burst and drench
what hides and disguises us,
as we experience, closer, closer,
on the long road,
the little things: love, death.

II

It is good knowing that glasses
are to drink from:
the bad thing is not to know
what thirst is for.

Antonio Machado

In The Harbour

Dear D., I'd like to explain things here.
Cows are content to chew close to cars.
Salty and sweet, so many bodies
of water, so close, they touch shoulders.
The sea lifts you up with a passion –
the swimmer sleeps well when it's over.
My house, or part of a house, has diamond –
shaped glass, all colours, in windows.
Light spills over wood floors at five,
six in the evening. Across the harbour,
fifteen maples live at the golfcourse,
the old guard, jovial, surveying
the evening. Wet mornings are vases
brimming with dahlias. How could I not
have this great, this enormous hope?
I'm here in this town, not somewhere else.
Though things split apart, I guess you heard.

Faces we couldn't recognize
were our own.
That's how I see it.
What I didn't see
is still there, a boat in the harbour
I don't want to board.

These days brush over me
like a light blanket.
They beat down on me
like midday sun. I'm tired.

Or else I'm up for days.
Then I'm white sand burning
while hours burn down and ash
blows into the sea.
Every desire is a second chance.
Every risk, a second, shimmering.
Even loss shines
in the dark. How can I make this any more real for you?
Visit. I'd like that. Or write. Love, C.

How It Was

Child, let me tell you how it was. I came down those hills
on a slippery road and each time there was the sea, open,
greeting me. Sun held me and then, turning,
I swerved toward water. Ice and foam. I surrendered caution
to your father's waiting hands and
he caught me. Nova Scotia. January. My first time here.

Choke cherry bushes tangled
with thistles and mud coloured birds
scattered in the yard. Bursting on stems –
hydrangeas. So much space.
Your father split wood. And each evening
perfume of dusk rose in the pink light. There was the heat
between us, yes, but it was the heat of fever
and it left us thirsty. An explosive
kind of craziness hovered over us
like a raven.

*

In the morning your voice
drifts from your bedroom – your plans,
your explanations. When you sleep
rapture flutters beneath your eyelids. I feel it
when I come into your room.

You like to put one thing inside another,
pennies in a sock, soldiers in a cup,
and when I lift a cushion, wedged in a crack,
a broken doll wrapped in a scarf, waiting to be rescued
and placed inside something else.

Here, where the ocean is a mirror
behind my house, I believe I can hear my fate,
if I'm quiet enough. The plans
time has for me. What's left behind.
And what's uncovered when I least expect it,
hidden inside something else.

Caleb

Little boy crying because you think I've left
without saying goodbye. Crying
because you're alone in the car too long.
Sucking your thumb, pulling your ear.
Saying, 'Daddy says I won't suck my thumb if I drink milk.'
Lying in bed at night calling out, 'What should I think about?
I'm thinking scary things.'
Your skinny body in t-shirt and pants that fall off.
Wanting one more kiss.
Asking, 'How do you cry? Do tears flash out of your heart?'

Remembering all the names in a book we read months ago.
Asking, 'Did Daddy say we could stay at his house two nights?'
Piling toys on your bed saying, 'This is a boat.'
Singing, 'I have a penis.'
Telling me, 'Aduki beans are very tasty, aren't they.'
Saying, 'It was good to see you after the adventure at Daddy's.'
Wanting to know what happened when you were 3 years old,
2 years old. Saying, 'Shh, I have to hear what my heart's saying.'

Caleb, there was never a time you weren't with me.
I missed you before you were born.

My Future Calls Back To Me

I make no plans.
Yesterday I bought peaches.
I cut my son's hair.
The damp days I swim through
wait to deliver me. There is no future.
That said, I expect great things to happen.
I want to be old one day.
'What is the farthest place away?' my son asks.
I don't know.
How far will I go before I turn back?

Luke

1. I was tired and wanted quiet
   and you kept talking – you were only three
   and then, calmly, you picked up your orange crayon
   and drew a line across the oak table.
   'You're a pain in the neck,' I shouted grabbing the crayon
   and you looked down, your hands open,
   and said, 'I didn't hear you.' Then your mouth quivered,
   your eyes filled. 'And I do such beautiful drawings,' you said.

2. We're playing hide and seek
   and it's dusk and you and Caleb
   climb down a hollow
   and lie on a pile of leaves.
   When I glance down
   you're both lying so still,
   you look like soldiers in a trench. 'Come back,' I say.
   'Game's over. We're going.'

3. I say, 'Everyone loves you, Luke,
   do you know why?' And you, bored, say,
   'Because of the look.' I keep telling you
   you're beautiful! I must stop this perpetual kissing.
   But you don't seem to mind, do you,
   Luke who moves fully
   into laughing and laughing.
   Luke who keeps getting the wonderful joke.

Women At Forty

The days are theirs to move through
where all motion smoulders.
Clothes slip off them
and colours fill the lakes of their bodies.
Sun dissolves in hair.
No matter what they carry
the world holds them in its grip simply because
they have a way to loosen love.

The way they open a blouse, for example,
or open doors, certain, in some room
of some wonderful adventure.
They believe in their bodies,
believe love can deepen,
houses will be cheaper,
on each walk they are growing younger,
in each new house the foundation will be stronger.

Behind them, a world that moves
too slow. They no longer seek
what they do not want, or flaunt
what they begin, or search for those
who do not need them. They know what,
besides time, haunts sleep,
what is moving away
and what keeps coming closer.

Women at forty are the end of summer,
lakes swollen with warm water,
eel grass. They border fall
where they will have to say goodbye
to long evenings. Now, at the height of the year,
nights chill slightly, nights filled
with summer skies – the Big Dipper,
the Pleiades, bodies blazing.

They still believe
they will not relive the past,
though some days, yelling at their children,
they know already they are their mothers,
with the old aches, the old affinities. They do not yet know
even old women search. That one day
the future will be dark and will swim behind them,
unhanding them.
They will be cold in winter, cold in summer.

Through A Slit In The Tent

1. The woman walking turns her head
        as the car slows down. A man digging
  in a field stops to watch her,
        skirt blowing against her leg. *Woman.* Even the sound
  is private. A lake too black
        to see into. But the word itself is
  rust red, the colour of barns, or maroon, an old house
        at the end of the road, the porch light on. Inside it's dark,
  the woman who lives there has gone out,
        perhaps to the water. Night beats against her
  empty door, as the man who's passing
        feels his heart beating faster. He knows
  this woman, remembers, last time,
        how she looked at him.

2. Another time
        the man lies, restless. Night enters
  his sleeping bag. Through a slit
        in the tent he sees stars touching each other. Out there
  a black hole in the galaxy pools with light. A summer night
        arches against it. There's a smell of salt
  as when the wind is in from the sea.
        The night is narrow. Beside him the woman
  moves her leg. He wants
        to touch her. He wants
  'to find Venus in a diagram of the female anatomy.' Even the pull
        of the earth around the sun, he thinks,
  has to do with those times, late, late,
        when a man enters a woman.

3. In tents of sleep a woman
            stirs, giving the man the feeling
    he is in the dream she is having. The wind
            that touches her shoulder
    brushes his mouth. Night fingers
            the shells by the water. This is what brings
    the sky to the ground and makes night slide
            onto the sand. Outside the tent, a glissando of water
    moistens a deep, splayed channel. A bud
            presses against a leaf.
    A woman *evokes* ... No.
            A woman *reveals* ... No.
    The sky is down on its knees
            giving up all the rain inside it.

    This is a story that begins at the end.
    You have to walk slowly back (as the man will do)
    in the dark. The woman inside the tent stretches her legs
    as the first curve of light softens the Eastern sky.

On This Ocean

On this ocean,
we have both entered
my body which is not mine
but the world spinning so fast it seems
not to be moving. You pushing into
that Mediterranean, that Indian Ocean. In Africa
mud is warm. Water spills over earth, steaming.
So much sun. Your body –
a meadow to lie down in,
bury my face in. Your face
all wanting and knowing. That face.
You grabbed clumps of earth, mangled flowers.
I left my names, my underthings.
I lay in the middle of the open field,
my mouth open. My mouth open.
I do not know if I traced your body,
boulder, strong root.
We are going deeper into our own world
so that I hear, from the other world,
water slapping, wind, birds calling.
There is never enough in this earthly light.
We find the well we can go down into,
all light and echoes,
drink from it,
hide the path leading to it.
You've taken my secrets.

You've placed them inside you.
The sun melts under your tongue,
and blackberry juice, a drink
flavoured with sloe.
I memorized you, warm breeze
grazing the tip of me.
How big are we, being the world?
Can we take the moon into our mouths?
I am floating still on this return,
water flowing up from under rocks.
When I wake in this boat of light
I am the boat. I am lighter than water.
The floor is water. I am returning
to the other world.
The other. World. My hand
reaching you.

If I Had My Way

If I had my way I would take you
under the shadow of trees
and tell you things. I would take
one of your hands
in both of mine, below hills
where moss clings
to the curve of rocks. Something in us
is unfailing. As light
as sun through water. Though water
is reckless. Waves crash. From them
the last drop of mist contains
more life than you need to populate a world.
The world is shivering. Listen: Your voice
is a river spilling into an ocean, or night
rushing into a darkening sky. Like coming home late,
the house dark. Who is waiting but someone you once knew
and were not expecting
and were hoping to see again. And there's wine
and cake left from last night.
In the most unexpected places,
you're waiting. Years from now
we won't remember the pact we made: to confess
nothing, not to lean
over the edge of the world.

My children are asleep and friends
have gone home. It is all
enormous. I'm forced
to start small.
If I had my way ...
But each life requires love
it cannot use.
Yes, it is me.
It's the invisible me who won't forget
and who you hold without touching.

What You Need You Continue To Need

When I close the door, I still don't think this will happen;
I've lived for years with the feeling
that happiness has consequences. But in the end
there is something that goes through one person into another.
Like something you can taste, it floods the mouth
when you don't know it's entering.
Or, like clothing that sways
when you're naked underneath, its power remains
the wearer's secret. Inside dark,
the wound that surrounds you
needs my hand, my mouth. An open thigh
is more than invitation. It's all feeling in this chasm
where we find ourselves and there's – what – grace?
The walls are witness. And the floor.
We don't sleep at all
that first night. Pain teases us
and in its teasing, partly, we are pretending.
When I pull your hand away
you will not remove it, my mouth
not big enough for your fingers, your tongue. I can't deny
this contract we make, this privacy
between us. I rub my mouth
into your life, this stiff insistence and even
shame is exciting. I like the way
you oppose me. How masterful
you become. And I am no longer
tired, your mouth on my body
questioning, answering.
Your words, unspoken, insist, 'It's all right if you're

nervous, if you're beautiful, if you're not beautiful, if there's
a scar on your thigh, if you've been reckless, if you're
almost crazy.' What I repeat
in my head, in a mania of prayer is 'I want him'
as you ask me to turn over, my hunger parted,
my face in the pillow as I lift myself up
when you enter as if something this deep
could fill us both, could go on forever.

For All The Impermanence

Like that love-lies-bleeding I transplanted
to a warm spot in the garden
we must hold this feeling carefully.
It's new to us.

I must say repeatedly: 'this is'
so I can feel the words in my mouth,
see how they warm me.
For frustration, for messiness,
we must be good hosts.

Apart from what we wish things happen.
Sometimes people board fast-moving trains.
They build a fire by a lake
and stand in front of it to break the rush of cold wind.

It is our weakness that part of us
is behind us and part beyond –
we're not yet in sync
with ourselves.
And then, like a conjurer,

destiny becomes an avalanche,
an invalid, a walk up a hill.
In the light of that sunset, I see you
in the frame of my open door, sad, sad.

For all the impermanence
we must act, as you walk in, as you sit down,
as if we had all the time in the world.

In the Kaballa it is written
there are three things we must do in this life:
plant a tree, write a book, have a child.
We must, in one lifetime, be born a Jew.

On your return, I will be waiting for you.
I will tell you I have begun,
in the garden, planting, planting.

Rituals

The rituals of love are intricate,
passed on by invisible signs – more often overheard,
stumbled upon. To enter, the young girl, the older woman
must slow down at different intervals. As this –
you turn me into ale
and drink me. I am the hollow of a violin
echoing sound. I am water, then a piece of silk. Sun
exciting rivers. I know the right from the left.
The air vibrates. When I am a woman again
I must be careful. My right hand on your right hand.
There's a yes. And a yes. And there are no's.
Secrets that will not release themselves. A vial
full of tears. Herbs steamed in tea.
A circle drawn on the earth
beaten 108 times.

This: words like broken glass. My name gentle
in your mouth. Silence
ominous or tender.
If you were Orpheus,
you wouldn't turn around, you're that strong.
All trees that stand up straight
boast and boast

of a steadfastness. Shriven, daring, undaunted,
I'll take anything
given with the whole heart. The whole
unbroken, broken heart.
If we want to stay
there are ways. If we want to leave,
the dead will show us how.

III

It's this way:
being captured is beside the point,
the point is not to surrender.

Nazim Hikmet

Think of the hands as breathing,

Opening, closing. Think of
The emptiness of hands.

Donald Justice

A Woman Speaks To A Part Of Herself

You've seethed inside me for years, brooding. It's time we spoke.
Though I've no proof, I believe it's you who broke
my health, left me tongue-tied, a broken sieve.
You force me off the road, hurt my children. And I give
free reign. A minute's long enough to know
you nearly killed me. How could I think
we could live together, will against will?
The car climbs its slow hill. A bird dives into water.
What's left – a sifting and sinking of borders.
I could confess so much but it seems a shame to share
my deepest thoughts with – who are you? A switchblade? A red
flare?
It's time we severed ties. So much is riding on your whim.
When we part, it's you who must go, must leave behind
what's not yours at all, you who have my name, my face,
my body, my thoughts, my anger slow to unwind.
I know you. You've left the best me
untouched.

Breakdown

Like a lake filled with ice
that creaks and groans,
that's how love filled me.
Days were heavy as trees sheathed
in ice; calm lost
in the snow, on the highway. So much sound.
I was eighteen.
Love invited me into the world
the way snow invites an exhausted child
to enter its whirling and blowing.

No sleep. Cigarette after cigarette
I became invisible.
How could I escape?
They locked the door on the long ward.
Outside, the city glistened.

In the hive, ghosts of bees singing, but mostly
dark. On the ground, frost.
When nights chilled, breath was sweet, stinging,
life bringing deeper life.
But it was having mine nearly lost
and then returned that I learned
everything, even death, is alive.

Her Kind
for Anne Sexton

I. All those nights your husband saying, 'Yes,
you're a good girl' like prayer before sleep.
But there is some pain no love replaces.
A woman like you breaks a cup once it's filled,
careless with pills, psychiatrists.
But not afraid to be blessed.
A night sky has many faces. If I'm sad
it's because a woman like you, fevered and chilled,
braver at night, seeking warm caves in the woods,
is always seen for what she lacks.

II. Anne, I take walks on rocks
that hours later will be covered by sea. It feels
like a forbidden place, where secrets lie.
A charmed place. A woman I know
takes rocks from there,
drills them with a diamond bit,
and emptied, they become vases, bowls.
Hollowed, they are more than themselves.
Anne, nothing stays empty,
nothing stays secret for long.

III.   Anne Speaks

'Under water, light moves differently. It bends,
unfocusing. It doesn't
illuminate. In this life, the tasks we choose
are busywork. Training for a harder chore.
I remember this: by waters well fed, aspens
leave their shadows wedded to the ground. What we are given,
we are given to love.
In ninety years you, and everyone you know,
will be dead. Then you'll know
what I know now.'

IV.   Does time move back
giving us wider berth
until it disappears? Until we see who we are.
You must have come to tell me things.

'I'll tell you this: I see the beach
you walk on. It's beautiful, so many stones.
I'm not the water you look into. I'm standing
at the portal of the cave. One day
you'll be amazed how deep you'll go.
You haven't yet told your story.
You called on me to tell you this
and I can: It's time. Nothing will pull you under.'

Where

I want to go – where? To Greece
to the island of white houses and blue
roofs. A week in Cuba. Even Cape Breton
with its trailing music, its Celtic allusions. But my schemes
don't catch. All my ambition
poured into travel books. I'm tired, not so much
of the cold, how it's stored in the blood, but of conquering
nothing. Bold as I am, I can't surmount
this flood. Something has happened
to my heart. Its meridian passing through
yearning, obsession.
'Don't leave without me,' I cry. To whom?
What has a head on it
but not its own? What goes up the chimney
down? How much is 5 Q and 5 Q? Wind is perilous and moody
playing its pipes in the long grass.
A voice says, 'Your ticket's ready. Your job
is to intercept it.' *Pillows. Umbrellas. Thank you. Thank you.*
Planes take off. Boats leave. Cars travel
all night, headlights boring into dark. Stains on the table,
like continents slipping into water.

Nine Oceans

Light, that transparent ocean,
streaks through curtains
and wavers on the ceiling
as if in morse code.

*

The ocean's oily green
washes ships at the wharf,
blues at the horizon. The best days contain
space that surrounds
a single ship travelling.

*

I leave my window open
to the garden: radishes,
slipper orchids, sea salt.
But even if the only thing to enter were ...
Are you mine?

*

This town was put together
like a child's game: a school
next to a jail, with
letters missing over the door. All this
by an ocean.

*

It's easy to forget:
what lights the way,
burns. The ocean snuffs out
the morning with its fog.

*

Surely we lie down
with what is most luminous and enduring
and it rocks us as if
the ocean were bursting with a sense of itself.

*

All loneliness
makes its way to the same place.
This is why
the oceans are so large.

*

I turn quickly
thinking a car is behind me
but it's only the ocean
echoing farther and farther out –
Are you mine?

*

The labyrinth is opening
for those who walk with their heads down,
for those who have not yet
seen the ocean.

Real

Lie on top of me.
Make me stay perfectly still.
Something is burning inside my body.

In the dark
I'm tempted to make alliance with yesterday.
Do not let me.

Say, 'This is what I like.'
Then I will have to see you,
preference makes a person real.

This life is going to do what it wants with us
and then it will slip from our breathless bodies.
Hold me. Keep me here.

The House I Moved Into

'Oh please don't go – we'll eat you up
we love you so.' Maurice Sendak

Here the foundation. Here the front hedge.
    The flue choked. The roof sagging.
        On the second floor
                an open ledge.
This is the house I moved into.
    Static. No station. Where night keeps to itself
        the smell of a furnace
                burning past mistakes.
This is the house. Steps creak
    to a third floor. In the early hours, sleep is the word
        I repeat between myself and myself.
                With calm broken
the world breaks.

Then the clamour.
    Longing, by its very nature,
            pounds on the walls.
    Anger sounds its single note.
        The cockatoo calls. There are dreams
                forgotten upon waking
                and early hours where, waking,
                I'm tangled in the same sentence.
                What is so terrible
I can't remember it?

Where the wind bangs the door shut,
even the worn down wood feels tender. Each creak
repeating its name: obsession, obsession,
obsession, obsession.

At The Café

I observe myself
as if I were a stranger

waiting to be invited to my table.
Outside – a park boys are disappearing into

and a night I've walked through
for hours and hours.

I never lingered in the dark
unless I thought someone would find me.

The night's all smoke and ash. Damn
the coals this wet. You were hard to draw

into my circle of words.

Aubade

'There is no happy music.'
    Schumann

This music
does not give up its secrets
easily. Wind rushing leaves
could be a brush sliding across a kettle drum.
Water vibrating
could be skin from that drum
as sun skitters rocks. Like a bow deepening sound
shadows deepen at the bottom of trees.
And this burning – clearly it's not in your control
who'll set fire to desires crackling in you
like tinder. In hours
forests have burned
and trees have gone down crashing.

As for me
I have taken something into my heart,
a wild mocking thing that goes on and on
and I cannot listen. Strains that enter this chamber
have a muffled sound and there's a click
that oppresses me. How difficult
to sing a simple song, though God loves
simple things. This fluttering – so many birds held back.
This music – caught in the night, like mist
snagged on the branches of trees.

The Sadness of Windows

They shoulder each other in old houses, these windows,
catch light as it fades
and store a glint that draws us in.
Behind this we house our fear

though it's just a trick of light
that turns a blowing branch
into a grasping arm,
just the shudder of wind, the panes empty.

Outside our window the river mirrors a white barn, floats
lights up and down its other side.
It sucks in grey sky some days,
leaves a blanket of fog to cover its deeds.

There are doors no one will open for us,
windows we are forced to look through,
out past our own reflections. Windows that look
into someone else's past. And in some lifetimes

we are always looking in. In some rooms
we always feel trapped. Nothing we do
is enough. No one we love
fills us. Like dark inside water,

some longing never leaves. We don't know the cure,
just the wind's cold shoulder. Nothing can shutter
the sadness of windows. Their long endurance.
All the light they let in.

Repair

The wing back chair looked sturdy enough
except for a gash in its side. Only in class,
as I remove wads of stuffing and straw,
strip it to wood and springs, do I see
the chair is alive. I pry panels off arms –
brittle bones seventy years old or more. Wood splits
as hammer lifts nails. The chair, naked,
is in my care.
Outside it's snowing. The sky is black.
Someone mentions a husband, a wife. We're hammering
tacks into material. What if this tenderness
is about to burst into flame? So much exhaustion!
On the way here I got stuck in a snowdrift, the road
from Oakhill to Dayspring is slippery.
I had to get out and shovel. Everything is in our care:
roads, chairs, quiet. Among all this –
sitting together or in different rooms –
one person is always trying to find the other.
In the cold. In the most terrible storm.
So many people I couldn't be still with.

The blue chair is in a different living room now
than when it needed work.
It sits this morning, sun on its shoulders,
part of a stillness, a quietness,
time rippling out, patient,
patient.

Breaking

No one will see his face
as I saw it: open, open, open,
closed.
Love caught us up like water
and gently eased us toward each other.
Beneath us the current, strong, dark.
Let me not forget the words,
like a trap door sprung open,
a noose tightening around me.
Shouldn't life be cleaner than this?
Clean windows? Radio that works?
When I left I could take nothing with me,
I couldn't leave anything behind,
the low tide quickly rising.

Sometime in the last two months
I noticed a change. I seem to have broken
through the surface, to another, cleaner place. Hours
gazing out the window, the light warm, flushed,
a tinge of pink flooding the field.
Whatever we do or don't do,
we live, finally, by shining. Some nights
we hold nothing back, our light is that strong.
We started this journey in a country

that has disappeared, though the trees,
the lake, they remain. And the sea's
unpredictable heaving. Wherever you go or don't go
I speak from experience.
It will be a long, long time
before you break free.

Fear Ghazal

In the form of a black moth,
fear flew out of my body and went off, free.

Old age walks towards me. I want nothing
to do with it, like a teenager ashamed of her mother.

Once, if nights were cool and a voice said, *go in*, I would.
Now nights are cold and I still go out though voices tell me *stay, stay.*

Father, do you hide your tenderness?
Are old age and illness all you've been given to face your death?

Having laid your hands on it you know it's ice. But courage
disguises itself, the way a wild ocean delivers ships.

Soon The Sea

What seems to me most my own
    are walks I take beyond shops
        where wind carries the smell of salt.
    By wharves where no one walks
I've gone out in low tide,

beyond the point.
    And though it was the middle of the day
        I was eerily alone and I thought
    I should turn back. This is as far as I'll go.
But I walked all the way to Mason's beach

on a field of stones. Water yielded up
    ruins – minarets of shells,
        bits of dulce and kelp, vermillion, ochre –
    shreds of Persian rugs.
Sea grapes the colour of mustard.

Down the road flagpoles rocked in their stands
    and birds called out. But I don't watch birds. I don't see
        well. I don't read signs. Strands of leaves and grass
    elude me. But trees, with their rough bark,
their broad limbs, are, for me, personal. Like water.

These past few weeks autumn forced itself on summer
    as if to say, *I'm going to marry your daughter.*
        I'll go to your funeral. We're going
    to know each other. The nights,
trembling, unfold. They invite me like an open den;

something wonderful waits
in that dark room of silk and brocade. But in the morning
just wind blowing over a stretch of sand.
The sun is out but it's cool. Soon the sea
will be too cold to swim in.

Five Doors

1. The tide comes in, swollen,
    inching over rocks. Here, the full day
    meets the broken day, and the hour, full of light,
    holds the sea in its arms. If blue is hope
    it is all around me.

2. In this frame, there is more weight on one side
    than the other, surf pounding
    off rocks into openness,
    spaciousness, so that in the end
    one is just beginning possibility.

3. Let's believe, in time all desire reaches its goal.
    I wear my loose and beautiful dress.
    After the storm, water shows itself
    unbearably tender, haunting.

4. Honour, relinquishment.
    I plough soil again and again.
    Who doesn't want what's underneath?

5. When night comes, something speaks
    from that soft, fragrant wilderness.
    It says, *the heart is not a door. But it opens.*
    We feel in the dark for the hinge.
    The body, our great ally,
    knows what it's here for.

Signs

There are always signs: a blue heron, that lady of the marsh,
stepping her way through the swamp. Or standing
so still. When she spreads her wings she rises
with such awkward grace, into the deep cool of the evening.

Into the clear surface of the evening
breath rises. Each living thing can only repeat,
with a gradual loss of strength,
its own story, in its own voice …

We're all hungry.
We all need to rest
our burdened body
on the warm grass.

We can fail at many things
but there are some things
we can never fail at.
As slow as we go

life moves even more slowly and one day,
as we give ourselves to what claims us,
will take us down
into its rising secret.

IV

Instead of grief, there are the hands of the clock
taking time slowly into its arms.

Nancy Kricorian

Starting

I have to begin without you
on my journey toward you.
I've rested a long time. You'll be surprised
how strong I've become. Like that tree
pushing itself out of dark each morning,
a pale pink light behind it like the pink of a well loved dress
just put on, and then later
it fades, limb by limb, until it is just a mirage of itself,
sinking back under its dark cover.
It is such a large tree, and protective, marking my place
as I make my way.
There. Your laugh comes out of my mouth
at the most unexpected times. You surprise me. And your words
come up in certain conversations. I blush
as I claim them. Though no one knows
they're yours. Not even you. You're not here.
Which is why I must begin
without ceremony, without invitation.

People forgive
so much. With you I'd wake from dreams
of falling backwards. I had to go to a place
where I could feel, directly in front and directly behind,
enough space for the spirits that protect
to keep their vigil. And I was protected
in the cool rooms, in the airy rooms.
I'd smell salt from the sea by the windows.

How long have I acted
as if everything could wait till later?
No. This fierceness was sent me. For the real work,
the long journey toward one another,
where one person begins and another ends
does not take place at the border of the body. What does God
want with us anyway, the light like gold
spilling outside our door, a door surely we are meant to open.

Corresponding
for Bill Matthews

The world is moody and round, Bill. But it's not the world
that picks a quarrel with me. The other way around,
as if I might sail off it.

Expecting to put the manuscript in the mail and
confront a blank desk, that exhilarating combination of
terror and possibility, like the 'on the edge' mood you
described.

I haven't seen you in 9 years. In letters I tell you
day to day news – I'm tense. It's not quite warm enough
to swim. By December, month that buries light, I will have
forgotten the smell of salt. Between us, a thousand miles.

Carole, I don't know when I'll see you again,
but in the meantime ...

'Ear that listens to the wind.' That's what sailors
used to call their sails. Recently, you've sent poem after poem.
I'm no longer the student only. How lucky, this quiet shift.

You go toward what's difficult when you can,
but when you need to, you lay low.

In a field of wildflowers wind dies down. When it's cool
you take off your shirt and fold it around me, draw me close.
If, in this sheltered place, it grows cold? How far can we look
into one another's life?

One of the best sounds is the late night presleep
murmuring of a couple happily accustomed to one another.
Sometimes I think the secret of a long marriage
is second marriage.

There's a vein of sadness running through your letters,
and bravado and an effort to cover that sadness.
Through all we've shared, you never once said, 'This pain,
this need.'

Your job is to write more and more like you. Your poems are …

and here you say something wonderful. I'm a beat-up ship
and you're the wind some days, and you're an anchor.
Should anything happen to you …

You've got such a whole and healthy heart, how could
your tile break in the mail?

Ours the hour when the table is cleared, before the meal is
cooked, when school buses rattle by,
the children not yet returned. When light from outside is enough
to brighten the white washed room, before other chores
demand us. The house quiet. I hold your letter in my hand.

This letter right away to answer your loving concern. And
that concern matters, yes.

Ours the field uncut, the wind streaming. You've wrapped me
in towels as if I've just risen from the bath. You hold
the door open.

Judith

What we decided on the front steps
eating jujubes. How many children we'd have, what our husbands
would look like, that it was good
to have money. You pointed out
it would be awful to be a has been.

Out west winter grain has failed. People are farming sand. This
life gives its gifts – hunger, indecision – the seed of the
wheat.

In sixth grade Mrs Tully told us
not to hold hands, to sit with our legs crossed.
One Sunday we screamed into the phone, 'Your son Ted
made us pregnant.' Next day she pretended
she knew who had called.

A valedictorian, you won the prizes. But in highschool,
one year, you stopped eating. And you could be mean.
It always surprised me. Still, I thought you were great,
applying to Radcliffe. A popular boy asked you out.
'Even when you touch his penis, it's not embarrassing
to see him next day,' you told us.
We knew you were meant for great things.

At first the crazed are hesitant to snip a flower
from the public garden. In the end they tear up
whole bushes. You must not be surprised.

I knew you became a doctor. A year early, an accelerated programme.
But when I wrote to a friend and asked how you were,
how could I have been prepared to learn you lost your license,
you live with your parents, they have custody of your children,
you work as a waitress in a topless bar.

There are stories told by people who imagine
they are in the same room, observers
who want to get the scene right, but who never once
understand the tone. Versions tinkle like coins in a jar.

Let's meet in New York. I'll fly down. We'll have dinner in some
cafe. Drink beer. I won't
show you this poem.

Visiting

Visiting from New York you tell me
you drank too much when you were younger, your wives
wanted to be taken care of, I'm too lenient
with my children. Behind us,
that great solitude of childhood
we just barely emerged from. We still don't feel
like citizens in the world
of the adult. When we return from our walk
we sit on the beach, watch the shoreline.
Near the sea I'm often reminded
of things I once knew and no longer know.

In the garden we till seaweed
into soil. Patches of sun are cloaks
angels have discarded. It's warm
where they are. Where they are
the past and future
are seen in one place. You rake leaves,
put up storm windows. You want
to do what's right. But you're angry, that's what I think
the heaviness surrounding you is. Beneath us,
the hard ground, unyielding.

The present demands
we enter the house of memory
with our eyes open. We give anger
its rightful place. Larry, when you're back in New York
I wonder if you'll do something crazy. I don't know what
I can do for you, how I can place
something in your hands you'll choose to open.
I sit on the rocks, the sea shimmering,
the book of water, unopened,
at the bottom. Each day
brings more than it takes away. I look hard
at what I'm left with.

Favours

The dead tree has been leaning
ominously toward my house for months.
Silas comes by when the kids are out, an expert
on such matters. He likes my red dress.
'Carole' he calls as if in pain
as his chain saw hits a metal spike.

'To hold up the dead trunk?' I ask.
'No. They used the tree as a pole for something.'
Later he's pleading, 'Use me. Use me.' His wife's
away.

He's good with heavy tools. Bluster and words. A wild,
playful antelope escaping.

Debts, dreams, the whole string of knots.
Silas goes to evict his tenant.
'I wouldn't want to trade places with her,'
he tells me.

This time of year
hummingbirds are up from South America. They come to the feeder
darting, sipping, flying away. They need to eat
every six minutes.

The tree down, there's just wind
against window.
Towns are like sex. You want to see them
as a whole
but each of us is left tidying things up
in his or her own rambling house.

Back and Forth

From the station a whistle blows
as a train pulls out from Halifax to Montreal.
To Saratoga. To New York. And some of us
make our way home. And some travel back
and forth. And time is fluid. But the ghost train
goes in only one direction – back back
back back.

It tells us
what we had here, and what we had
here. But we don't know where the truth lies.
There are musty rooms
on the other side of nothing. Dark alleys
locked in the negative. Beyond zero
cold allies itself with cold.

Go on. If you borrowed emptiness
from your lover
how long would it take to pay him back? What
would you be left with? Nowhere
the cool stream, the hummingbird flying, sun
seeping through your blouse. Not this memory, not this letter,
not these kisses. Nowhere
silence replacing danger. The body never
disengaging itself from
longing –
those notches of a ratchet wheel.

Of course things do come from the opposite direction
on those bright mornings, with our expectation
of a life more honest, more startling, always better.
Though we can't see

into that future. Lucky
aren't we.

George at 88

What am I doing here? In the other bed
a man I don't like. It's so hot

in this room. I hate how desire
to look over the edge gets drained away

by ordinary chatter. No buildup. No revelation.
I can't get anyone to open windows. Even in the summer

when it's cold. I just don't like being tricked.
I can't hear what the nurses are saying

and they won't repeat themselves. But listen –
more and more I find myself

closer to the edge of something. Like when I sold windows.
If you look long enough at anything

you can see right through. Though I never wanted to look
too closely. Had this life not forced me,

I might have always turned away. I was afraid. Though less afraid
than my wife.

The children have their own lives.
There's so much I regret.

Give me a map. I'm here. Everything
is where it shouldn't be.

Our Favour

The older I get
the less confusing things seem
and smaller. I take up
such little space.

I used to climb the top of buildings,
balance.
At the most dangerous times
I didn't think I could lose anything.

I wore tight clothes and high heels.
I wanted to race
and could barely move. Hope, that dangerous thing,
took refuge in my skirt.

I lived in a dream, like a child,
though I wasn't a child. I was an idea of myself –
my mother the one
who never had children.

I saw my mother today in the hospital,
an old woman,
82 years and so young,
her eyes the eyes of a sad girl.

One day I'll be an old woman too and know,
not about desire, but what lies hidden in desire.
Some days I am handed a key. Some days
the answers are at the bottom of the page.

All I can do is go deeper.
That's where everything is stacked in my favour
though time, which gives and gives,
has us on its own terms.

A Person Forgets

Somehow a person forgets cruelty. Its details
get assimilated, an ache
in the stomach's pit. Impossible
to forget kindness.

I remember having to move and friends
opened my messy cabinets, packed my dishes.
Those days the boys rarely saw their father.
I had fallen into fear, tired, aching, as if into a pit.
I didn't know how the disaster started or if it would end
but friends said it *would* end.
So much kindness rescuing me
when I've sold myself short.

These days, when I want to hand something down
to my children, something stunning
and glittering like freedom,
it's my father's face surfacing before me,
his tired shoulders, his old coat, so familiar,

like Joseph's, that visionary, whose brothers
sold him into slavery. In the end, of course,
he forgives them. They shake hands.
No hard feelings. The coat
that marked his privilege
is gone. The colours now
are in his dreams.

Does pain make us aware? Or kindness?
There's a thread running through me
that gets snagged in the past,
most of which I don't remember.
Even in my dreams I know
it's my own hands that must protect me,
my own visions that tell me
how things begin and end.

Where I Stand

Counting currency is the business of the future.
We are not concerned with that.
It is another room we face – and look:
we are already made into the stranger
by the way we hold ourselves,
the way we walk in. The ex-husband and ex-wife
watch us. In the dull light
people are mistaken
for the weight of their shadows.
Outside, walkers are eager for summer weather.
But there's only a grey sky balancing
over clods of dark earth
and wind fretting salty water. On the black roads
a dust of snow blows, lambent, smoky.
There are colours in the sluice
where water and ice slur,
water that is held back passing through the gate.
The day is porous and lets other days seep through.

But that is the business of the past and the past receives us
cooly and makes us feel like outsiders.
'Now will my husband dwell with me
for I have borne him six sons.' We know, of course,
the answer. In this room we measure time by shadows
and by misadventure and mistake.

When I close the door I call the closing
the dream of my forgetting.
If something does remain, it is the click of the door
and grace for grace and, on good days,
a desire to walk quietly and feel the fullness
that enters this wintry place
before I get tired and turn back.

Cannon Cave, The Ovens

1. I am standing in Cannon Cave looking down
   into milky water. A cannon sound booms
   as water shoots through.
   I've heard stories, how years ago,
   at low tide, Mi'kmaqs paddled canoes
   up into the cave's mouth.
   At dusk, water phosphoresces and jewels green,
   stalactites sweat. But only once, the first time I came here,
   did water address me.
   I was with you and you asked the ocean to speak.
   You said – I won't repeat it. You know what happened
   after moments of silence when water roiled faster and faster.

2. The first time we do anything
   we're right there on the surface. We don't need
   to go any deeper. But these days
   on walks, I knock inside me
   and it's strong and hard as oak,
   and scented, light.
   I don't know how this change occurred.
   There's no longer that fear in me,
   that well I couldn't see into
   where water churned and when I did look down
   it was dark and dense
   and cold as a lidless black eye.

Show Me

for V.S. Naipaul

Sometimes I look at my own world and discover
it almost doesn't exist. So much veiled.
Some days
the world thrums in me
with its inner consonances. And silence
fills my body, just as gold of the day
is stored in the dusk.
I have always been faithful
to that silence.

Look, I tell myself, you are on the same path
as the exiled, the disenfranchised.
You have committed yourself to something
you don't really understand.
Still, I know I am going to be all right.
Horses gallop toward me
as the sun is setting and will reach me
before night falls. When I ride one of those horses
I will know how wind feels
when it rides the ocean.
I have forgiven myself for my constant clash
with the future. And for the times
my body was a mined field
and friends were reminders
of roads that veer off,
of paths that circle in the woods
getting wider and wilder
until they disappear in bog.

Is this light seeping up from the page?
Is it stronger than cloth or smoke?
'I know what gives you courage.'
Can I say that to myself?

With Lights Off

On the wall shadows of a tree waver,
leaves blowing. Soon I'll get up. Soon I'll wash,
the chill will lift. Our cat Blackie
breathes deeply, going about her morning sleep.
How busy things are this still.
Last night, waking, turning on the light –
just a black sky outside. With lights off –
white streaked the horizon as if,
beneath night's darkness,
something luminous and alive and soft grew.
Soon I must return what's been lent me.
Already there's a chill in the breeze.
Such small things make their pleas
to us. So small they vanish, untreasured.
How much have I mistrusted or misspent, or lost?

Next Month Snow

Wind reaches up through my skirt
mocking a thin slip. Nothing
wants to be excluded.

Surely love, that condensation of feeling,
forces us out in all weather, as anyone who has stood in a blizzard,
coat open, knows.

It's November. My third autumn
in this country, ending.
Next month, snow.

Yet for all its coldness,
there's a tenderness in winter too, making us cover
what we can no longer bare.

I dig holes, plant bulbs in hard places.
Quiet holds me. Nothing
penetrates as deeply.

In winter, the belt of Orion loosens.
A blue star at his heel glows.
Wind wills its way

into the coldest water
while the ocean struggles for breath
bursting the cords of foam around it,

the ocean weighted heavily upon itself.
But oh the wind
twisting off the sea,

the mist rising through trees.
Death as close
as the mist.

I had not, as Buddha suggests,
meditated on death,
though what else is as faithful?

What else,
pretending to let us go,
holds us so closely?

Here, where night is a prayer in God's heart,
dark, full of yearning, I'm left holding
what, for so long, I held back.

Notes

In *Through A Slit In The Tent*, the quotation in stanza 2 line 11 is from the poem *Little Whaley, Pawling, N.Y.* by Marianne Burke.

The phrase 'It's time we spoke', in a *A Woman Speaks To A Part Of Herself* is taken from Charles Simic's line, 'It's time you spoke' from *The Inner Man*.

In *Aubade*, line 22 is from Leonard Bernstein's MASS: 'God loves all simple things, for God is the simplest of all.'

In *Favours*, 'Towns are like sex' is a variation of a line by V.S. Naipaul, in *A House For Mr Biswas*.

In *Judith*, stanza 5 and stanza 7 were influenced by Janet Malcolm's New Yorker article, 'The Silent Woman,' written about Sylvia Plath, 1993.

In *Corresponding*, the italicized lines are from William Matthews letters.

In *Show Me*, the italicized lines are from letters V.S. Naipaul wrote to Paul Theroux.

Publications

Poems have appeared in the following journals:

The Canadian Forum: In the Harbour, With Lights Off, The Little Things, For All The Impermanence, How It Was

The Fiddlehead: Prayer, Luke, Her Kind, Judith, Women at Forty, Repair, Breakdown

Malahat Review: A Slit In The Tent, George at 88, Scanning an Afternoon in Winter

Event: Travel, Looking At Houses

Antigonish Review: Soon the Sea

Grain: Our Favour, Visiting, Back and Forth, A Person Forgets

Prairie Schooner: Hansel and Gretel, Fear Ghazal

League of Canadian Poets Anthology, 1992: Next Month Snow

Windhorse Review: The House I Moved Into, At The Café, The Sadness of Windows

Windhorse Reader: Choice Poems of '93: If I Had My Way

Thanks to the Canada Council for financial assistance which made it possible to work on the poems in this book.

With much gratitude to Don McKay for his great care and skill. I couldn't ask for a better editor.

Heartfelt thanks to Dennis Lee, who, with his generous response to my work, was invaluably helpful.

To the wonderful poets: Alexandra Thurman, James Warner, Lianne Heller for their comments on many of these poems. I so appreciate you.

And to Bill Matthews, always, thank you.

Carole Glasser Langille, originally from New York, now lives in Lunenburg, Nova Scotia. She is the author of another book of poetry, *All That Glitters in Water*, and the children's book, *Where the Wind Sleeps*, a Canadian Children's Book Centre Choice for 1996-1997.